Peaces

Poetry and Prose

"*Peaces: Poetry and Prose* is a lovely, highly descriptive collection of everyday aspects of life transformed into art. Ramanda gently and lovingly grasps the reader by the hand and shares her vision of what we all see but now know through her beautifully different lens. *Peaces* is an enlightening page-turner that is hard to put down."

—**LEWIS W. DIUGUID**, Journalist, Author, Lecturer, Diversity Facilitator

"These poems and compositions are, in a sense, the declarations of an African-American woman whose own humble beginnings were her greatest teachers. There is beauty, spiritualism, love of family, and determination to overcome pain, and most of all, there is joy ... lots of joy. They are expressions that transcend differences or privilege. They are the writings of a woman who could be that caring Sistafriend to anyone."

—**PETER MORELLO**, Associate Professor, Broadcast Journalism; University of Missouri, Kansas City Department of Communication Studies

"Ramanda has magically taken mere words and united them in a way to make them dance, sing, and cry as they descriptively unite in a way that only our hearts can truly interpret. In *Peaces*, a voice is given to the voiceless in ways even they could not accurately script. Bravo on this written work of art."

—**DR. ALICIA R. DICKENS**, DBA, MNLP, Associate Vice Chancellor, Metropolitan Community College.

Peaces

Poetry & Prose

RAMANDA

HIGH BRIDGE BOOKS

HOUSTON

Peaces
by Ramanda
Photography by Rick Wheaton.

Printed in the United States of America
ISBN (Paperback): 978-1-946615-62-6
ISBN (Hardback): 978-1-946615-50-3

High Bridge Books titles may be purchased in bulk for educational, business, fundraising, or sales promotional use. For information, please contact High Bridge Books via www.HighBridgeBooks.com/contact.

Scriptures marked NKJV were taken from the New King James Version®. Copyright © 1982 by Thomas Nelson. Used by permission. All rights reserved.

Published in Houston, Texas by High Bridge Books.

For more on Ramanda, visit www.iamramanda.com.

Contents

Foreword

From the first time I met Ramanda at her job inter-
view with me at the University of Missouri-Kansas City, I
knew she was special. She had all the qualities of a smart
and determined young woman who was on the path to a
great future. She displayed an image of kindness, profes-
sionalism, and genuineness that is rare in today's society.
Although she has a sweet, quiet demeanor, a fire inside her
lights up the pages as she expresses her thoughts through
writing.

Over the years that I have known her — as an employee,
graduate student, mother, businesswoman, community
volunteer — I have rarely seen her angry. She exemplifies
grace, dedication, and a will to succeed. As I write this for-
ward to her captivating book, I get the opportunity to share
with her what a special woman she is and how her drive
for success influences others around her.

Peaces is a book that powerfully and metaphorically
gives the reader insight into how our lives can be in *pieces*,
yet we can still find *peace*. It reveals that although we may
not see it, there is a greater power within us guiding us
every day. Often, we conclude that we can never pick up
broken pieces, yet we find ways to get back up and become
stronger on the other side.

In vivid form, Ramanda shares the journey of child-
birth, motherhood, loss, friendship, and more. She writes

with a definite understanding of how to overcome obstacles, offering a narrative that is not simply a story but an exploration. The eloquent poetry is evidence that Hicks' voice is found through her writing—something that she always loved to do despite having to juggle work, family, school, and other responsibilities. This book is unique and important as it gives insight to experiences of the challenges of everyday life and how we can be inspired by our environment to overcome any obstacles that come our way.

Readers will delight in witnessing her passion for stories—and how she weaves each reader into the fabric of each poem. Powerful and passionate, each poem in *Peaces* is both emotional and relatable to the reader. Each line is a glimpse into the soul of a woman as she reflects on her life journey. Ramanda Hicks has written an amazing book that is both personal and powerful.

—**Dr. Kimberly Johnson, Ed.D**
    Director of Special Projects
    Office of the Chancellor
    University of Missouri-Kansas City

Acknowledgments

First, thank you to my Lord and Savior Jesus Christ, who broke me, reassembled my broken peaces, then poured hope and purpose back inside. Through your love, strength, and protection, *Peaces* went from vision to provision.

To my children: Thank you for your many sacrifices, hugs, jokes, and laughter. Without you, these peaces would have never come together.

To my family: Thank you for giving love that is complicated, fractured, unconditional, and blindingly beautiful. Big Ram—I heard you when you said, "Someone needs what you have right now."

To my friends and sistafriends: Thank you for helping me carry a few crosses when I misplaced my crown … you know who you are, and I love you for it.

To my teachers and mentors: Thank you for challenging and encouraging me over the years to weave a great story— but most of all, to never, ever stop writing. May your seeds continue bringing forth fruit in due season. (Ms. Turk, Ms. Franklin, Mr. Hutton, Lewis Diuguid, Glenn Rice, Elaine Schlozman [deceased], Stanley Banks, Maureen Maginn,

Patricia Scaggs [deceased], Peter Morello, Kevin Mullen, Carol Koehler [deceased], Rick Wheaton, Pete Wilkerson, Doretta Kidd, Mel Tyler [deceased], Natasha Ria El-Scari, and more...)

Introduction

This body of work is a reflection of the hopes, dreams, successes, and failures I have experienced spanning several decades. Through the death of my unborn son, divorce, various forms of abuse, unemployment, and frayed edges of sanity—I found myself again. Though the mental, physical, emotional, and spiritual journey was long and, at times, painfully lonely, I was not alone. Jesus kept me when I could not keep myself, offering grace and hope while counting my tears and patiently understanding exactly where I was. Each poem is accompanied by an actual personal prayer that helped me live through a crisis; these prayers were also answered. Captivating images by Emmy Award-winning photographer Rick Wheaton offer you gentle, guided beauty while walking through the pages of my life. May hope and grace continue to abound in all of your many peaces!

I See Giants

I see giants in the land.
They camp 'round about me,
Pitching tents and countless
Like dunes of sands.
Their fortress of walls looms
High overhead, casting guilty
Shadows where headless bodies
The lions fed.
Their mouths hang open,
Spewing lies and faithless discontent.
Nouns and verbs form unholy
Unions walking down the tongues'
Slippery isles.
Broken promises drift
Aimlessly in the wind,
Rushing everywhere yet
Going specifically nowhere.
Land carelessly as they may
On fertile ground, ripe with opportunity,
Her womb does cry.

I see giants in the land
Who wear my pearls around their necks.
Priceless nooses in the hands of infidels—
Unworthy, unapologetic, unknown—

Are the gifts we gave,
Trampled under split hooves
Of the unclean.
Dedicated in earnest to all
Their wicked ways.
To the hills, I cast a lonely gaze
Beyond the height of his head,
Knowing the sun again will rise
Just like it falls.
A pebble, a stone, a prayer—
Summersaults through the heavens,
Landing in Goliath's crown,
Leaving a lasting impression
As his gangly pride topples to the ground.
The shadow that once loomed overhead
Now casts woeful pathways on the ground.

I see giants in the land.
Yet I take spoils
With pearls in hand.

Father, help me cope.

Too Far to Walk, Too Close to Run

...the race is not to the swift, Nor the battle to the strong, Nor bread to the wise, Nor riches to men of understanding, Nor favor to men of skill; But time and chance happen to them all.

—Ecclesiastes 9:11 NKJV

My spirit was turbulent and restless against the abandoned sheets on the right side of the bed. Interchanging thoughts running through my mind and going nowhere like a deconstructed highway. A fan next to my bed blew the pulsing heat from between my toes protruding dangerously close to the edge of the mattress where the sheets could no longer contain them. I had already wrestled with the "why," but tonight's meeting was a raspy "what now?" Too young for a female mid-life crisis and too broke to pay any foolhardy man no mind—at least no time soon.

The walls stood at attention, coated in white like towering flags of surrender, beckoning me to just give up. The room in the air seemed to be filled with only my air, and it was suffocating, dizzying. After fighting primal urges to unleash my wrath upon a Judas tide, the still small voice called me to run. At 6:30 a.m. on a sultry Sunday, the streets of Blue Ridge lay like an open welcome mat before me, the crickets and cicadas singing praises though worries unknown. Morning's sleepy eye gently blushed an overcast sky without giving over its hiding place. My gray jogging shorts and red tank top were the right clothes to wear to this service. Just me, God, a hallowed street, and a prayer.

As I began my journey walking, the direction without a destination leveled in front of me, waiting for a command. But I could only walk toward the sun. My prayers quickened with the cadence of humid breaths between rapid steps, now turned strides. I continued past the corner and right at the yellow flashing light. My eyes lifted to see only the road before me: "Thy rod and thy staff comforted me." Each seductive rise and fall of arching hill climaxed, released, and prepared me for another. I thought about looking back to see how far I had come, but I couldn't. So I kept running on. Tears now streaming, though my salty breasts heaved with the heaviness of uncertainty.

The road got wider, but the walkway was narrow, ending about a half mile after the last house on the right. From that point on, I knew I would be alone with my thoughts, my fears, my prayers. Too far from where I started to turn back, too close to run away from whatever came next. Tears and sweat stung my eyes as every fiber in me begged, pleaded for answers. So I kept walking through the road now lined with thorns, thistles, and cattails on a path already set for me.

The scent of morning lake water flooded my nostrils, though it was not in the script. Now that I was over two miles from home, my haggard pace slowed to a crawl as I contemplated stopping again. Just as I wiped my brow and looked for a sign—a cloud, a flower, a tree, a thorn—a voice in the wilderness of my heart began to speak. My legs ached with faithful fatigue—too far to walk another step but too close to run away anymore. A sparkle of light caught my glance, but I couldn't see what it was until I took a few more steps. Shattered diamonds dazzled the surface of the lake's tension. The road once winding had now become straight, revealing the destination.

Lord, help me find the strength to bear, to heal, to live—and move on.

A Bag, A Box, A Purse, A Pile

A bag sits on the floor in the corner of my bedroom with its wrinkled, shiny black skin. Its sides reveal invisible stretch marks around its bloated belly, full of things that are too small and things that never fit in the first place, but I kept them anyway. A thin red plastic bow tie loops tightly around its neck, leaning against the wall like a broken-down pimp with all the time in the world to solely solicit me.

A box sits on the floor in the corner of my bedroom, filled to the top and overflowing with past-due bills, invoices, and miscellaneous receipts. Each small slip of paper a witness marking time on my soul's carbon ledger. Their white, yellow, and pink tongues protrude tauntingly from the cardboard corners of its mouth, spitting accusations for a tentative tomorrow, already 90 days past due.

A purse sits on the floor in the corner of my bedroom, two gently worn leather handles with tiny fissures across their arched backsides. One handle concedes defeat, releasing its hold from one of the gold-tone metal buckles. After carrying load after load, it finally snapped under the strain like a brassier with a cup overflowed. The outside zipper pocket will not close, spilling everything it knows—a careless side-chick with a place to put small, meaningless things. It knows it is good enough to be used, but not solely good enough to complement any decent wardrobe.

A pile sits on the floor in the corner of my bedroom like a lop-sided junkie crumpled up in a heap made of greasy cotton-blend t-shirts, holey mismatched socks, jeans worn threadbare between the thighs, and a stale, day-old washcloth. Oh, but only if she could just stay clean. Lying there within plain sight of indifferent church-goers for the last two weeks, merely a stone's throw away from the bedroom gate shouting, "Unclean! Unclean!"

Lord, help me to grow and mature spiritually to handle what lies ahead.

Delicious Sin

Darkness blankets time and space, covering our hidden nakedness and burning desires. Summer's seductive breath caresses the back of my neck with trembling anticipation. It happened before and likely is not the last that I repeatedly hear the words, "It's mine." His rustic, woodsy cologne intoxicates my will in his embrace while working his fingertips across my lips. My eyes closed, yet his face ever-present beneath each flickering lid like a private picture show. He walks slowly, skillfully … through my midnight garden of thorny rosebush brambles.

Muscular arms gently part intertwining branches, exposing the soft, vulnerable bud to all that is forbidden for those leading into lost temptations. A dark path now exposed, yet no light may escape its open sepulcher. Babbling brooks and streams cannot contain his opaque reflection, saturated with morning dew. His rope-like locks drape effortlessly past his bronze, armored breastplate. Vineyard grapes hang low, swinging slightly from side to side as the earth beneath us gives way to spasmic tremors and heaving aftershocks.

Lying motionless within eternity's glimpse, emerald blades blanket the ground and brush slightly against our barren flesh, fresh with morning dew. Moist, full lips dipped in sweet nectar glisten effortlessly as the sun rises, cresting beyond the hills and valleys of my mound's horizon. Each warm, heavy breath exchanged in our midst rushes swiftly through my nostrils, filling my lungs with suffocating pleasure again and again … and again.

My mind mumbles unspeakable obscenities, a testament to the ecstasy evident between us. The sun exposes our delicious encounter, laced with sin's ungodly stench. Gently flaring nostrils and thirsty eyes signal initiation of a second wakeup call. His python-strength arms stretch and tighten around my waist, while repeatedly piercing my soul with his hooded dagger; heaven help me. Complete surrender consumes my will to envision consequential depth beyond this moment. My eyes search the heavens, desperate for acknowledgment, or perhaps eminent condemnation prefaced only by the heat of hell's lapping flames.

A sudden fiery jolt electrifies my senses and slashes like lightning across my throat, ceasing all wind and song from within. Confusion abounds as I helplessly writhe and claw at the shadowy grayness looming over my vulnerable flesh. Chocolate wine flows effortlessly from the open wound across my neck, spilling liquid foundation on Mother Earth's face below me. Two windows slowly open one final time, filled to the brim and overflowing tears from death's ruthless baptism in delicious sin.

Lord, help me to be sensitive to your Holy Spirit. Bless (insert name here) and speak to (his/her) heart. I pray for truth and (his/her) deliverance.

Four Ladies for Lunch

One Saturday afternoon at a local bread and pastry eatery, four silver-haired dames met up for lunch. As I sat in the chair just across the way, tapping chronicles of my own life into the stiff keys of my laptop, I paused for a moment to indulge myself in observation of theirs.

They were all clearly past their fifty-mile markers, but of the four, one was undoubtedly the unofficial matron of the bond they all seemed to share. Silver, wispy crowns of wisdom swirled in curly patterns atop their heads. The youngest looking of them, clearly determined to deny age the rights to her locks, had brownish-colored hair with snowy-frosted roots. Their narrow shoulders heaved up and down in delight as they recounted personal stories of triumph and overcoming from days and times past.

As the conversation shifted from history to the present, each lady went around the table, taking turns presenting bragging rights of new grandchildren or proud accomplishments of their offspring. Their comfy cardigans and orthopedic shoes, paired with small cups of coffee and tea, provided just the creature comforts they needed for catching up. The third of the four ladies relaxed in her high-waisted jeans and white tennis shoes while her oversized brown purse waited patiently under the table near her feet.

Her back slumped slightly forward and pressed against the back of her chair as she smiled intently and watched friend-ship in the eyes of her friends. As I glanced back and forth between my glowing screen and the edge of my wire-framed glasses, the conversation shifted once more, this time to family lineage.

The second of the four ladies shared newfound information regarding the true origins of her family's lineage. She seemed encouraged and hopeful that now her family would have newer, more accurate tales to pass on. After about fifteen minutes of observation, their half-chewed ba-gels and flaky croissants were now finished, leaving just brown paper napkins before them, dotted with sweet crumbs left behind.

A slight glance at her watch by the second lady revealed that it was about time to wrap up their silver jam session. While they gathered their belongings and positioned them-selves to stand, two of them needed a little help—one with a rubber-tipped cane with four feet, the other with a guided elbow upward from the first lady. Soon, all four of them stood together beside the table, exchanging gentle hugs with arthritic hands and arms. Their varicose veins and freckled age spots had no bearing on the bond they shared across time and space. One by one, they formed an unoffi-cial line, the oldest being the line leader, and moved toward the exit not far away. Their shuffling feet and chattering giggles slowly disappeared around the corner beyond my sight, out the door and into the parking lot.

I rolled this experience around on my pallet of observations, wondering if my new friendships would one day become a sterling alliance like theirs. Or perhaps I was the fifth lady having lunch, uninvited and unaware.

Lord, trade my ashes.

A Letter to
My Firstborn Son

My son, my son.
My firstborn son.
I have so many things to say, so where do I begin?
Perhaps I start on my knees,
With hands open in prayer position,
Pouring unspoken words
From a weary mother's broken heart.
When you walk through the doorway in the hall,
I see a young soon-to-be man
Preceding the shadow of a little boy I once knew.
At age fourteen, your six-foot-two-inch frame
Begs to be the man of the house.
But only I know you are still afraid of the dark
Places in our home and in your head.
Your flawless adolescent skin glows
From hope's reflection,
A future bright with opportunity,
If not for the journey misled.
You stole my smile from the first suckling at birth,
And later borrowed your father's voice—
Shifting, shuffling, running feet first into manhood.
Sometimes I see joy in your eyes dance and flicker,
A flame replaceable only by rage and disdain for me.

Yes, until age eighteen, you remain my responsibility.
The breath I breathe is yours.
Red and blue lanes form highways for veins,
Transporting billions of your cells
Nourished by my molasses-colored soul.

I don't know how God is gonna fix this, but I trust that he will. Throwing my hands up and drying my puffy red eyes for the night. God is able…

Counting Tears

I saw a familiar man while at lunch today. He sat alone at a table near the window facing the sunny side of the street. When I turned to walk away from the cash register, his gaze beckoned from across the room, strangely drawing me toward the empty chair opposite of him at the two-seater wooden table. As I approached and stood oddly at his right side, my mind said from within, *I feel like I know you.* Our lips never parted, yet his eyes met mine and said, *Please, have a seat.* A white porcelain teacup sat upon a small saucer, supporting the steamy liquid contents before him. As I pulled the chair out and slowly sat down, gentle ripples bounced across the surface of the calming beverage to the edges of the cup and back again toward its center.

Slightly weary from a long morning's work, I placed my belongings—which included a black laptop bag and a small leather purse I bought at the thrift store—beneath the table near my feet. He did not seem to mind my presence. In fact, it was almost as though he had been there waiting for me to arrive all along. The salt-and-pepper-colored nest atop his head formed a cloud of endless wisdom. His skin was dark with a smooth leathery finish like weathered hide in the Sahara sun. His eyes were deep galaxy pools and innumerable stars, greater than the sum of our universe. Gentle creases framed the outer edges of his mouth, full lips the only barriers to contain unspoken life. The plain, short-sleeved, white cotton t-shirt he wore glowed like fresh, driven snow as penetrating rays filtered through its thin woven fibers from behind. Then there were his hands, neatly placed around the outside of the cup, fingers slightly interlocking at the tips. I noticed random scars on the left and right, tattooing history from times past into flesh that refused to forget where they had been or what they had done. Oh, what secrets they must securely hold.

My eyes panned the room's width for no one in particular before returning to his warm, watchful gaze. In that moment, the essence of eternity, time, and space stood still, completely silent and peaceful. Miscellaneous worries piggy-backed on my shoulders or stowed away in my computer bag were immediately forced to be still ... they knew. As my tired eyes settled back on the tabletop, a cleansing sigh escaped through my mouth and nose, so heavy I feared I just might exhale my soul. Without warning or solicitation, I began to share random facts and details with the familiar man, including incidents from the morning traffic-jam commute, the weather, my children, a looming foreclosure, catastrophic divorce, church hurts, and more. This emotional emesis went on for several minutes and did not stop until my heart dry-heaved one last time, then there was nothing left. Newfound shame forced avoidance of eye contact.

I blinked once ... full ... twice ... blurry ... thrice ... blinding burning tears filled two open wells. Then, just as the first torpedo escaped its ocular prison, gravity's greedy grasp pulled it closer toward the table's surface. Before it could land, a scarred right hand swiftly, yet gently, reached across the table and caught it. His fingers closed around it securely, then, methodically, he opened each finger individually to expose his sunken palm and a single diamond with absolute clarity. Sunrays ricocheted through its translucent prisms, casting dazzling rainbow bridges in every direction. Astonished by what I just witnessed and too shocked to continue crying, the familiar man leaned slightly forward toward me and whispered, "Seven hundred forty-four thousand, three hundred and twenty-one." His free left hand traced the outside of a small, tan lambskin satchel he carried in his lap. He gently picked at the loosely tucked flap at the top as his hand disappeared inside. Before I had time to inquire, his left hand emerged from the small satchel carrying a red silk pouch of sorts, tied tight at the top with a single drawstring. The familiar man leaned back into his original position and used both hands to carefully inspect and balance the precious gem at his fingertips before discretely slipping it into the red pouch.

Year after year of misappropriated emotional funds yielding negative returns had finally manifested themselves as record-breaking dividends of tearful currency. His gentle gaze slowly reconnected with mine. A soothing peace washed over me from the inside out, the likes of which I lacked words to describe or comprehend. The familiar man inexplicably bore witness to every hurt, shattered dream, broken promise, and wounded discontent I packed away deep in my soul's basement, labeled in black permanent marker as "fragile." Without utterance, he explained why these experiences occurred and how each hurtful or inflammatory situation rendered my tears priceless.

Indeed, my wilderness experiences were necessary, and nothing I had gone through would be wasted in fulfilling a promise with purpose. He further explained how he tried to contact me for years to express his deepest love for me, but I was routinely unavailable, leaving messages unanswered or calls unreturned. He loved me for years from a distance (distance I had created, though not his preference), patiently awaiting an invitation to one day come in and dine with me. A solitary tear pooled inside the narrow ridge of my right duct, distorting his smeared image in my mind and painting my heart's broken canvas.

The familiar man leaned slightly forward, taking in a slow, deep breath, and exhaled a calming wind between the coarse whiskers of his full beard and mustache.

Though my heart was heavy, I still count my blessings in that all of my children were able to be here with me, happy and healthy. That is a Merry Christmas. Thank you, Jesus!

Test If I

I sat in broken pieces on the hard, wooden church pew with barely enough strength to remain upright as they handed me my firstborn son. Too small for his own full blanket, they swaddled him in a crocheted fragment made by his grandmother and sat him in my lap. Silence. His eternal cradle covered in white fabric and traced around the lid with white lace, its total size no bigger than a shoebox. The impression from its chilled bottom leaving a rectangle-shaped shadow on my grey skirt. Everything in me wanted to hold him one last time in my arms as my womb cried out to eternity, pleading for this bitter cup to pass sinful lips not his own. It seemed as though heaven and hell had a seat alongside my anguish, casting lots to determine if I would completely lose my mind or, worse yet, deny God altogether.

And on the day I left the house and drove less than a mile from home to pick up a few things for my daughter's birthday, my divine destination was altered again. Cresting a hill, then headed downward toward the three-way intersection, a sedan approached from the opposite direction and abruptly turned right directly ahead of me without warning. In the twinkle of an eye, the choice to minimize a broadsided impact to them meant running completely off the road, so my grey van careened down into a gulley and wrapped around a tall wooden utility pole.

The tremendous impact cast the van's loose contents from the other rows directly into the floor of the front seat, though my Bible remained wedged open and undisturbed firmly in the windshield. Red and black verses reflected off the glass and into the heavens, forming a protective shield in the absence of prayer. Consciousness escaped me momentarily before being gradually awakened by the sound of high-pitched sirens, not from emergency vehicles but from deployed airbags forced to my face and absorbed through my ears. All five of us frantically rushed to nearby hospitals for immediate treatment. My entire body went into convulsions as blood filled my eyes; I prayed for forgiveness. Was this a test of righteousness to see if I was ready to die? Was this a test? I am still here.

I can make it. I will make it. I must make it, for failure is not an option. Beauty for ashes. Learning to let go. Lord, help me.

Running in the Reign

Against my better judgment and with all the best intentions, I headed out for an early morning jog-walk through my modest neighborhood. This was formerly a regular routine that somehow became very irregular until it eventually stopped altogether with the onset of cooling temperatures last fall. So, the challenge then became creating a new routine to regain my focus and "girlish" figure, one pseudo-suburban block at a time.

The air hung like fresh, wet laundry, heavy and damp with suspended purpose on the sky's overcast clothesline. Dawn pressed her sultry morning breath against every pore of my flesh, quickly nearing 100 percent humidity. Countless dirty grey clouds rushed quickly over, under, and past each other, like clumsy celestial SUVs during the morning rush with no destination. Birds stealthily camouflaged themselves within oak tree leaves and branches, their praises now reduced to barely above a whisper. Eerie silence, coupled with pregnant transitioning winds, warned me that her water was about to break; the rains were coming.

With one lap around the neighborhood and a few glances skyward, I convinced myself that there was time for one more before making the final few blocks back toward

home. But first, there was the gradual incline, which ex-
tended uphill and slightly to the right, intersecting with the
nearest cross street. My arches struggled to support the ex-
cess pounds unshed from last winter … or the winter before
that. Full-figured inner thighs rubbed together like smooth
brown flint in my black spandex yoga pants, nearly starting
a fire while the sensation of infinite bee stings perforated
layers of hidden cellulite. One foot placed methodically in
front of the other to the eminent cadence of fresh, falling
rain.

In mere minutes, a few lonely drops christened the edge of
my sweaty brow before the skies opened for complete bap-
tism by storm. A thin, blue V-neck T-shirt offered inade-
quate dry covering for me and my 4G cell phone, which
managed to shimmy halfway into the discrete crevice be-
tween my left armpit and damp breast. The briny mixture
of sweat, salt, rain, and hair grease cascaded down my en-
tire face, creating a stinging veil over my eyes. My glasses
were completely useless, so I removed them and placed
them into a simple hanging position with one arm securely
anchored in the bottom neckline of my shirt. Now that I was
visually impaired, houses turned to multi-colored moun-
tains and parked cars to stoic monsters with four black
teeth. The hot pavement before me became a flat, murky
ocean. My eyes scanned haphazardly across the rolling
heavens as I walked and ran across invisible waves.

The neighborhood, once a familiar place, quickly became
an obscure landscape. Every few seconds, I repeatedly
wiped excess runoff from my face, nose, and lashes.
Though I felt as if I were drowning every time I inhaled

these angelic tears, my frustration grew because I could not see. It was then that a still small voice spoke and reminded me that I did not need to see, "for we walk by faith, not by sight." Gentle, calming peace settled over my mind and spirit; I knew as long as I continued to walk in His reign, I would eventually arrive safely at the destination prepared for me.

© Rick Wheator

Lord, help me to have a spirit of gratitude and forgiveness. Help me to harness the love you placed inside so I can give hope to others—not hurt.

My Skin Does Glow

Beneath summer skies
Cloaked in midnight's gentle embrace,
I stand naked and unafraid.
Moonlight blushes soft white light
Across lonely surface ripples,
Chasing each other from bank to bank, undisturbed.
His stance behind me, a steadfast scaffolding
Lest I should waver, or fall.
My sacred silhouette bends and gives way to subtle sways
Each time the wind breathes to caress my flesh.

Lord, help me to be patient.

I Have Permission

My gaze now dry with prying honesty,
I clearly see truth abandoned by misplaced hope
And early onset denial.
Like a moon wildly spinning
In someone else's parallel universe,
Space and time were but thin filaments
Holding us together.
Destiny, a shiny, dangling ornament
On Eternity's Christmas tree.

As the sun would rise and fall,
There was no difference between the two.
For all I had become revolved around
A red, giant solstice I called you.

The light you once had
Burned out with supernova-like intensity,
Leaving a black abyss where love used to be.
With no sun left to circle, complement, or complete,
My trajectory seemed destined for tragedy.

It was then that I understood breaking free
Pushed me far away, into another realm
Where I could learn who I was and why I was here.
When I observed the new darkness,

I discovered I was not lost or alone at all,
Not a moon reflecting another's expectations,
But a drifting star trying to shine in a broken galaxy.

So I give myself permission
To grow, To shine,
To learn, To know,
To stop, To start,
To ask, To cry,
To lose, To find,
To hurt, To heal,
To bow, To kneel,

To rest, To hope,
To commit, To let go,
To deny, To accept,
And finally, above all,
To forgive.

Father, forgive me for trying to be what I thought instead of what you designed me to be. Repurpose me. Make me and my heart useful again.

Get Naked

If I was going to go through with this, there was only one way to do it … all the way—completely naked. Plumes of rolling steam rose to the top of the bathroom shower ceiling like moist incense in the gods' nostrils. Six lights framed the wide mirror across the top edge, five of which burned out individually long ago, leaving only one to expose responsible truths.

Licorice-colored skin and runaway gray hairs reminded me of the things that had changed, including remnants of youth's playful mischief hidden beyond jaded disappointments in frameless eyes. Faded stretch marks crept subtly across my breastplate forged by motherhood's iron hammer, battle scars earned from suckling infants as well as their father.

Sliding each bra strap off the edge of each shoulder gave me permission to exhale while unhooking each snug-fitting eyelet from behind. My blue printed boyshorts easily slid down past ever-widening hips, revealing graffiti left behind from four pregnancies and three children—each child leaving their own brandings.

As I stepped into the shower, the day's cares became liquid sin running down the drain from a relentless baptism. My skin longed for the same cleanliness sought by my soul. Hot streams of water slithered down my face into my eyes and mouth. Both palms laid flat against the wet, wailing wall, awaiting his search and seizure. I spread my legs equally across the shower's width, silently wondering and seeking answers for how I ever got here.

Lord, cover my heart with duct tape.

Half Past Midnight

The dark night breathes on the back of my neck
and caresses my arms, whispering, "Come with me,"
into the thickness of quiet skies.
Somber waves bounce against the pebble-laden shore,
repeating pulsating ebbs and flows of "yes, yes, yes."
Calming rhythmic strokes relay to the shore.

Electric stars peak through your bushes and trees
as jewels around sultry midnight's naked neck.
Remembering a time before passion suffocated
in confusing whys,
dreaming of diving head-first into a memory
beneath the dark, shimmering shore.

Cast your anchor.
Thrust your rod into the deep.

Lord, please help (insert name here) to come to you and humble his/her heart. Please help me to release the hurt, anger, and truly to forgive—even if he/she never changes his/her ways. Lord, please protect my children. Help them to always know that this decision was painful but for the greater good.

Breasts

Behold her breasts in all their various shapes, sizes, and forms; the extent of their power remains untold. In youthful days, they mesmerize boys and entertain the imaginations of men. Somewhat hypnotic are their subtle sways, which captivate curious eyes and fascinate malleable minds.

They possess nourishing strength for those yet unborn, protect quiet secrets, and can console a broken man's soul. An inherent cleft offers balance for heads they often soothe, comfort, and confide. Never mind her own silent tears shed between intervals of darkness and light. Fall as they may subtly in between the soft crevice, then gently disappear beneath, creating saline puddles in her underwire gutter. Silent disillusion whisked away leaves no evidence behind.

Near the front-end of midlife's crisis, small, ghostly black-and-white images appear on sheets of grainy transparencies; their sharp outlines contrast against grey truth. Malignant cells pepper the left side like buckshots from an isolated drive-by as she rests in steady surgical hands. He, too, leaves a tattoo, claiming rights to something he never should have owned.

Mirrors reveal only present tense, except yesterday they told a different truth. Her body grieves and mourns, clinging desperately to hope's phantom presence. Her breasts fail to define her womanhood, nor do they quantify her greatness. For today, her gentle courage lies not in belaboring a loss, but in championing the greatest treasure of that which remains.

Still. Standing.

Thank you, Lord, for my real friends, sisters, brothers, and my enemies because it takes them all to help birth what you have in me. Bless (insert name here) and comfort him/her. Give them peace.

Purple Requiem

Standing with her back toward me, facing the southern wall in her bedroom, she gently wiped away silent tears leaking from just beneath the frames of her purple-rimmed glasses. Both shoulders heaved slightly up and down in her short-sleeved black shirt as she tried to understand why Death had quietly committed to visiting her beloved betta while he was left alone.

An empty shoebox with black writing on the lid weighed heavily of fond memories and tall fish tales between her hands. Just before she placed the lid on top, my eyes caught a glimpse of the small scrap of white notebook paper. A date and the words "R.I.P. Purpleoo" were handwritten in blue ink inside a small clear sandwich bag.

In humble silence, we made the processional from the patio door and down the steps, wading through eight inches of fresh snow toward the chain-link fence at the rear of the yard. She led the short trek without voice, only screaming sadness in each footprint left behind. Carefully, I landed each of my steps in the hollow of hers, not too close yet respectfully distant.

Few thirteen-year-olds are well versed in grave digging, and she was no exception, as evidenced by the snow shovel and hedge trimmers she brought along. She took the gray snow shovel and cleared away a patch of earth about two feet wide. Now exposed, she stabbed the ground, repeatedly piercing the topsoil and flinging useless heaps of frozen dirt in various directions, creating a reasonably-sized hole. With each thrust of the bladed shears, his absence became more present.

In subzero temperatures, she eventually replaced the shears with her bare hands, clawing at the dirt and thin tree roots—her tears freezing as they christened holy ground. The rich soil between her fingers and beneath her fragile nails testified to love wholeheartedly given and love tenderly received.

Birds sing in harmony with every whisper of the wind, praising without ceasing, for He is risen indeed!

Notes in D-Sharp

The other day, I stopped by to visit with an old friend. When I stepped onto the concrete stoop at the top of the front stairs, a doorbell with a tiny burnt-out bulb failed to announce my presence; five gentle knuckle taps would have to do. He opened the wooden door and swung the cast-iron storm door outward, a warm smile greeting me just beneath his meticulously cut mustache. We talked about moments that made us laugh and dreams we conceived as students in high school, some evident and manifest while others we silently put to sleep. Decades had been kind to him, weaving his love for music in and out of his spirit, deep into the marrow of his soul.

Slowly, he walked across the room and pulled out the narrow bench at the pearlesque piano, taking special care to acknowledge the locations of four random keys stuck in depression. Turning his grey ball cap from the front to face backward seemingly transformed my friend into an unstoppable jukebox. When his fingers pressed down the smooth black and white bars, soft hammers struck the internal strings, and chords of pure emotion rippled across gently polished oak floors. I watched him time travel from the '40s and '50s through the civil rights era to the neon lights and funk of the '70s and '80s before lingering in hip-hop samples from the '90s. His voice drew songs from the hollow of a deep well only his spirit could fully comprehend.

Spring raindrops kept gentle cadence in cut time, trickling from flooded roof gutters just outside two sliding glass doors leading to a saturated patio. He rocked and swayed, channeling Motown vibes, turning the brass pedals beneath into brakes while our road trip went from Detroit to Chicago, then rested in Kansas City. There were no windows, yet I felt warming sun and wind caress my face. It only took about four feet of ivory and ninety minutes of freedom to remind him he mattered, his hurt was real, love transcends through music, and life marches on even when the rest of the world has no conductor.

These are his notes in D-Sharp.

Take this bitter cup, Lord, if it be your will. Nevertheless, not my will but thy will be done.

Moments

They are too precious to hold in our hands
And too finite to measure.
When bound together, they define time, create life,
Or carefully script final breaths.
Like vapors, they rise into the eyes of the Most High,
Filled with penitent prayers
Or tears and laughter.
They are the gateway swung wide
For girls to become mothers
And boys to trace silhouettes of men.
Ripe, tender fruit they are,
bobbing to and fro in the wind.

© Rick Wheaton

Lord, whatever it is that I am missing, please reveal it, so I am not sleepwalking and can operate according to your word and not fear.

Taste and See

*Inspired by Euge Groove (feat. Peter White & Tracy Carter),
"Rain Down on Me"*

Taste and see,
Taste and see,
Just how good I can be.

When the wind blows,
I hear your name whisper between tree leaves.
And behind every raindrop, I named your tears,
Suspending them in colored arches across the sky.

When Loneliness admired you from afar,
I gently held your hand.
Knights, though dark,
Came and went quietly before dawn.
But none carried my sword and shield,
For only I know your name.

Taste and see,
Taste and see,
Just how good I can be.

Your lips manifest the heart's decree,
Total adoration in my presence,
Alone in my embrace,
I surround you in love and liberation
As you call my name—
Not for all I have done
But for who I AM.

Your children were his and are mine.
Their laughter forms eternal symphonies,
Reigning melodies among heaven's host,
A language only a mother knows.

Taste and see,
Taste and see,
Just how good I can be.

When you are ready and not a moment sooner,
Allow me to love you
Without doubt, guilt, hurt, or shame.
My love heals in every warm embrace.
I desired your presence
Before Time conceived your face.

Come, dine with me.
Feast on a meal fit for royalty in the halls of the king.
Vineyard grapes fill golden cups,
Broken bread we share,
and together, we sup.
For I AM yours and you are mine.

Taste and see,
Taste and see,
Just how good I can be.

I thank God that the scab is starting to form on this green wound. I am tired of feeling like the walking wounded, fresh from combat.

Beautiful is the Dawn

Inspired by Brian Culbertson, "The Journey"

Dawn, the colored axis separating night from day,
blushes across the horizon's morning.
Roads behind me are much darker where I've been,
yielding to oncoming light of where I now go.
My path is straight.
Though I know not the way,
my way is known and set before me,
a journey I alone must travel.
I carry a small satchel,
my stride certain.
Every step rests securely
between a promise made and a promise kept.
He said He would never leave me nor forsake me.
I walk between hills and valleys,
surrendering no light to watchful shadows.
Moist dew anoints my feet from nearby streams.
I am rested, renewed, and restored,
walking toward fullness.
Therefore, I go (forward)
into the beautiful dawn.

© Rick Wheato

Lord, help me not to fall. Keep my flesh under control and stay kept like the "old-school-religion" folks would say.

While She Walks

Before she was old enough to crawl, she walked into my life. Full of joy, hopes, and dreams. Her cooing giggles fluttered around the edges of my ears like monarch butterfly wings. Soon, she could inch across the shag carpet floor with a few belly flops along the way, pulling herself up one fist-full at a time. She balanced and swayed uncertainly with smooth, immaculate knees. Her knees had not seen failure and heartache yet, nor had they experienced the shame of begging and disappointment.

Instinctively the time to walk had come, the steps of which could never be undone. From that point on, her hands rested securely in mine. Whether it was playing at the park, buckling her favorite shoes, or dancing in front of the television with her hand on an imaginary hip, she was never far from me.

Months turned to years, and soon years merged into a decade or more. From the discomfort of a straight-backed folding chair, I watched her glide across the narrow stage in the school auditorium, carrying the responsibility of generations past and present. She stepped with confidence and intention in her stride, for destiny awaits. They handed her a paper baton, then shook her hand with broad smiles and warm blessings.

It was not long before chaffing winds of maturing youth and adulthood attempted to strip away childhood's innocent afterglow. Whether caring for a sick parent or preparing a family meal, the atmosphere surrendered to her inner light whenever she walked into a room. Her smile made any burden easier to bear, especially knowing you were not walking it alone.

When loved ones amputated their agendas or severed relationships, she was a loyal prosthetic supporting the weight of my broken heart. Step by step, she walked with me toward healing and recovery. My cross became hers as we traveled the stony road together. Sometimes laughing. Sometimes crying. Sometimes nursing wounds from forty verbal lashes.

So, 1 gladly place offerings of love, grace, mercy, peace, long-suffering, and gratitude before you. The same riches were freely given to me while walking with my daughter.

Lord, thank you for your guidance and wisdom, even when I don't understand why things happen. I know (insert name here) could not be a part of what you are doing in me right now, but I praise you for raising me and keeping me in my moments of trial, weakness, and indecision. Help me be all that YOU said I am. In Jesus' name, amen.

Sistafriend

There are not many women I can call Sistafriend. You are a pink rose plucked fresh from God's eternal garden. You were placed in my life's glass vase to keep me company, dance between brilliant sun rays, and sway in the warm summer breeze.

My life sometimes went in all directions, like the petals of my golden carnation crown. When days were weary, you helped lift my spirit, drawing strength from living waters below your slender green stalk.

Prickly thorns others may have felt at times were there only to protect me when I could not defend myself. No matter the challenge, your leafy green arms remained lifted in praise, yet extended low enough to offer a hand to others in need.

Over the years, honeybees and hummingbirds circled in and out of both our lives. Though many took without giving, your blushing honesty paled in comparison to the love you showed me.

Sistafriend, may the beauty of your spirit never fade and the bond we share remain forever blooming toward the pink dawn.

© Rick Wheator

Lord, I am still a mess, but I am trusting that one day, this too will pass, and somehow, you will get all the glory! In Jesus' name, amen.

An Open Letter to
That One Girl

This is an open letter to that One Girl. The one at eight years old who stayed the night at her best friend's house and discovered far too soon what it meant to be touched by an adult in ways she didn't understand. She felt afraid, lonely, and ashamed, though the sins of the father were not her own.

This is for that One Girl who wanted someone to actually see and acknowledge her at school. But instead, divisive lines between the haves and the have-nots pushed her further into invisibility as others walked through a hollow shadow resembling her presence.

This is for that One Girl who wore extra-long pants to work, hoping that the off-brand name tags and splitting seams on the sides of her shoes might somehow go unnoticed by her coworkers. Only Jesus saw the holes in the bottoms of her soles as she knelt in prayer during her lunch break.

This is for that One Girl they said was too fat, skinny, thin, ugly, and boring. I remember the day you stood in front of the bathroom mirror and opened the medicine cabinet. Your eyes shimmered with tears as you reached past the antacids and took a handful of aspirins instead. You arose the next day, still seeking explanations for why you yet lived.

This is for that One Girl who made tiny incisions across her flesh like tic marks with a microblade. Rose-colored beads appeared on her flesh as if to release pressure originating from pain and disappointment hidden within. As long as you covered them under everyday garments, your new normal remained undiscovered.

This is for that One Girl who did not know what "Daddy issues" were since he was never around in the first place. She looked for him subconsciously over and over again in the biceps and bedrooms of handsome men. She hoped that one day, just maybe, someone would hold her unconditionally. Not for her body, her looks, or for what she could do ... but just to acknowledge who she is and was to become when embraced in safety.

This is for that One Girl who wore dark sunglasses and extra layers of foundation. The bruises he inflicted on her emotionally are visible in her soul's windows. She shields them from daylight, concealed from scrutiny and judgment. Her spirit and heart bear witness to badges earned in wincing patches of black and blue.

This is for that One Girl who dared to dream and speak life through her words, even when loved ones laughed and mocked her. Like a gentle scribe, she wrote lyrics down on a small piece of paper and wedged them between the last chapter in Revelation. As long as she could see them sketched in blue ink, they remained alive, real, and attainable.

This is for that One Girl. I saw the tears of your unborn and the grandchildren you will never have. Your womb now barren from bearing the weight of bad decisions full-term. Stretch marks lightly tattoo themselves across your hips and breasts but bear no fruit. Your lullabies pierce the darkness, hoping they might reach beyond heaven's gates and into the children's forgiving ears.

This is for that One Girl who tried to achieve perfection and found only bitterness, anger, and failure. Your heart's desire was to achieve great things based on the template society placed before you. When life happened beyond your prefabricated controls, there was no way to adjust, cope, or relate. Grasping at reality's frayed hemline, you only reached an open-backed cotton gown in a room with no windows, padded walls, and bolted-down bed.

This is for that One Girl, living in an abandoned house near the end of the block next to the drug house. A charred black square of fibers was all that remained where a welcome mat used to be. You crawled past boards nailed as crossways on the back entrance. I watched you seek holy asylum peacefully between rats and crumbling floors, patiently waiting for dawn to shine hope through a hole in the roof.

This is for that One Girl building walls around her heart made of designer purses, high-end shoes, fake eyelashes, and gold-tone jewelry. These walls block the sun from shining on your insecurities. What would happen if people got to know the real you … the one that chose a designer bag over a bag of groceries? What would they say? What would they think? Or would they even take time to notice the scared little girl who desperately seeks validation?

Who is that One Girl? She is the little girl, the forgotten young lady, and the older woman within every woman. She is not forgotten. She is eternally loved. She is bold. She is brave. She is beautiful. She is forgiven. She is unashamed. She is you.
She is me.

© Rick Wheaton

God is able to do anything but fail, so I will look to the hills (not my current situation) "from whence cometh my help," for "my help cometh from the Lord"! Selah. (Ps. 121:1-2 KJV)

Friend

Dedicated in honor of my dearest friend, Mary

What is a friend? A friend can be defined best as one bearing characteristics reflecting an image like unto our Heavenly Father. At different times in our lives, a friend may perform in different roles as life presents itself.

A friend will wake up to answer a phone call in the middle of the night to hear your concerns, listen to your fears, and count in her head silently the number of times you made the same mistake yet never condemns. All the while, disregarding glowing numbers on her digital alarm clock suspended in darkness across her bedroom. In three hours, she has to get up for work, changing shifts—yet again.

She understands all of your weird, quirky ways that make you special when others see abnormalities begging for conformity. A friend will help carry your cross to "the place of skulls" when the world mocks your efforts to stand as 40 lashes rip the flesh off of your flaws and insecurities, exposing your barren soul.

A friend knows when to hold you accountable at times you may have forgotten not only *who* you are but *whose* you are.

She helps you find a reason to smile past the pain of loss, regrets, disappointments, betrayals, and self-doubt.

A friend will call on the name of Jesus to cancel strongholds upon your life that could otherwise ensnare many blessings God has in store for you. Her obedience is grounded in the Word and often fulfilled through sacrifice.

A friend has the wisdom to love your children the same as her own or scold them on your behalf when absent. Her intuition has a wingspan exceeding that of an eagle to protect those entrusted to her care while carrying them to higher heights, so they too can soar.

Her hands readily build upon foundations of excellence, lending compassion as brick and mortar, erecting monumental relationships with others strong enough to withstand Time's often painful erosion.

So, I say again, "What is a friend?" A friend is one Fulfilling Relationships Inside Each New Day.

Thank God for friends and family who understand my struggle but appreciate my process in progress.

Memory in the Midst

In the midst of our joys,
our emotions run high.
Voices lift up praise
Beyond the northern skies.
Tears of laughter slide past our cheeks,
Reminding us of day-old dreams
Washed away in seven-day weeks.
Among those dreams, I do recall
A tempest at sea
upon a ship did fall.
No light, no warmth,
nor land in sight.
Just mustard seed faith
enveloped by night.
The words were faint,
yet clear to me.
Fear had closed my eyes
to how He'd delivered
The future to be.
Two knees bowed humbly
Submit to His will.
Two hands clasped together—
and the wind stood still.
Memories of repentance, deliverance,
and unconditional love

reminded me of strength
received from heaven above.
Eyes not open
Now warmed in His gentle glow.
Once I understood,
But now—I know.
Memory is to acknowledge
those times we call tests.
They are countless examples
of God at His best.

*We are all that we are
because of who God is! There
is none like Him! Not one!
Blessed be the name of the
Lord Jesus Christ.*

The Magnificent Cries

His sigh is the rustle of wind
Through the forgiving bow of leafless trees,
And when the skies turn grey
And clouds roll thickly with resentment,
Oh, the Magnificent cries.

His tears are the life in the trickle of reign,
And as humanity is consumed
And digested by the darkness of light,
Oh, the Magnificent cries.

His love is life itself and the grace that dwells therein,
And such ravenous heathens they are,
Run wild with no direction.
Oh, the Magnificent cries.

His wrath is every damnation
Never spoken into existence,
And though their ears were deaf
To His calming whisper,
His footsteps could be heard from generations past.
Oh, the Magnificent cries.

And with every head bowed
And every eye closed,
The outstretched hands close
And seal the fate of time.
Oh, how the Magnificent cries.

Lord, have mercy on us all.
Help us all to repent.

Beauty in His Grace

Though at times, the loneliness of the world tends to set in,
A backslider's withering faith is not enough to begin.
As heartache turns to heartbreak and the teardrops fall,
Lonely hearts cry out to One who has seen it all.
With filthy garments and the stench of disobedience,
The human soul carries the shadow of repentance.
Vessels that sail, both young and old,
Must be tried and fired with the heat of pure gold.
Lips once used for desire and tender affections
Are now used as instruments of praise and projection.
Why a wicked life was spared
By only a glimpse of His face—
No one can fully understand
The beauty in His grace.

Show me, Lord, who you have designed me to be. I submit to your authority and welcome your anointing in my life. Help me be disciplined and respect your grace. In Jesus' name, amen.

"He who dwells in the secret place of the Most High
Shall abide under the shadow of the Almighty."
Psalm 91:1 NKJV

Made in the USA
Coppell, TX
18 December 2021

68779031R00062